Wanderlust
AND WIFI

HOW TO NOT QUIT YOUR JOB AND TRAVEL THE WORLD

AJ Marino

ISBN 9781717834249

www.MeetAJMarino.com

Introduction

Once upon a time, there was a girl from Boston who had an idea. What started as a plan to stage an Eat-Pray-Love style discovery across 12 cities in 12 months quickly became a spiral up, down, and around the rabbit hole.

I wrote this book for a few reasons: to commemorate my time abroad, to capture my thoughts and feelings in the moment, and ideally, to inspire people (like you!) to find the confidence they need to start their own crazy journey.

When I was starting out, I practically begged Amazon and Barnes & Noble for a how-to guide on how in the world I was going to pull this off. I never found one. I did, however, find some truly fantastic books, mentors, and communities along the way, and I'm using this little book to pay that advice forward. I'm also hoping it makes your life a lot easier.

As I've learned to do when traveling, I'm going to set a few ground rules for your reading of this book:

1) Leave your expectations at the door
2) Take what you need
3) Leave what you don't

PS I don't have a mailing address for hate mail.

Chapter 1: What Kind of Traveler Are You?

If you picked up this book, there was a little corner of your subconscious pulling you towards it. A secret desire you may not have even realized you had, but your brain was pushing you to discover. Or maybe it was the fabulous cover art... well, you're still reading for a reason! We all have them: those thoughts that you want to reveal to your best friend at 3AM or write in a journal but are too afraid to say out loud. Lucky for you, I probably already know your secret - because I've had those thoughts too.

Allow me to introduce the voices in your head. You may not recognize all of them, but I think once you see them, you'll know. I promise, I'm not a psychic - the truth is, we all crave adventure to some extent. We are all curious about living outside of the norm. Figuring out your intrinsic motivation for wanting to travel up front will help to guide you on the more technical aspects. Don't worry, this isn't going to be a bunch of psychological babble, just some basic storytelling I hope helps you realize you're not alone.

The Explorer

I grew up in a small town south of Boston. For comparison's sake, by "small," I mean a suburb of 18,000 people, but the homogeneity of my 98% white, Irish Catholic immigrant community made it feel a whole lot smaller. Growing up, I was never exposed to diversity. Everyone looked and acted the way my family did - except in one area. Luckily for me, my mother was born and raised in Puerto Rico and had grown up traveling the world with the US Navy. She would talk about far away places like Madrid, Naples, or Seoul as if they were neighboring towns, and she made me wonder if I'd get to see them one day, too. Living in such a closed environment, cities around the globe seemed more like photos in a textbook than actual destinations with living and breathing people, foods, and cultures. It's one of the downsides of the now widely-accepted, first-world necessity to keep children stable and comfortable in their youth - we rarely ever get the chance to explore until we're adults. Once we get here, we have all these hopes and desires, and a whole lot of fear and ignorance holding us back.

As I got older, I started becoming increasingly curious about the world around me. I would remember reading novels about time travel and replay Disney movies like Mulan and Aladdin, imagining myself running around those real world locations one day. It's what makes us all repeatedly share videos of unreal destinations on Facebook, longingly study the maps beneath beautiful Instagram photos, and add endless countries and tourist attractions to our Pinterest bucket list.

I know you've done at least one of those, if not all three - and why? The number one reason people long to travel is simply to experience the world around them. We crave the knowledge of how the images inside of our head actually feel, look, smell, taste.

Do croissants really taste better in Paris?

How does the salt air of the Caribbean feel on my skin?

How tired will I be after hiking to the base of Mount Everest?

How loud is the din of a souk in Morocco at midday?

Those questions may seem childlike, because, well, they are. Ever seen a video of a child in your life practically running away from their parents just to see what's around the next corner? The desire to explore is one of the first real feelings we experience the second we learn how to take our first steps. Your reason for traveling may simply be that one desire - to see the world for the first time. You don't want to see the confines of a resort, ride a segway around city sidewalks, or only see the two sides of your own country. You want to see a photo of the world and instead of drool, remember exactly what it was like.

The Patriot

Okay, admittedly I'm a bit of a history geek so the name of this inner voice has nothing to do with the major league NFL team (although I am from Boston, but in order to keep you reading, we'll ignore my team loyalties for now). When I say "Patriot," I am instead referring to the folks on the winning side of the US Revolutionary War. As a quick refresher, for those who weren't embarrassingly invested in American History in high school, the Loyalists were the folks who wanted to stay part of England, and the Patriots were the ones who craved **independence**. In today's world, I see those who travel and break the norms as the modern patriots of a work-life balance revolution, and those who stick to the norm as the loyalists. One of the biggest reasons to seek adventure is because you crave that scary feeling of being independent from the standards and expectations you've been living in your whole life. Travel puts us both literally and figuratively out of our comfort zone. Heading out into the world of the unfamiliar will test your patience, your confidence, your knowledge of maps, and your ability to laugh at yourself as you roll with the punches. It's probably going to suck in the moment, but the learning experience will paint it as something you'd never want to forget.

Going to school in the relatively small city of Boston, I used to hate visiting big cities like New York. Despite its grid outline, I was always overwhelmed by its sheer size and opportunity, and how many new and strange things were hidden in every corner. After my first four months living abroad, I came home and visited a friend in the Big Apple, and suddenly everything changed. I was easily navigating the streets, smiling at local business owners in store fronts, and it hit me: I had become comfortable with being uncomfortable. New York was no big deal - at least everything was in English! I started laughing in the middle of Chinatown, which earned me a few weird stares, but that just made the situation funnier.

This won't resonate with everyone, but for me, I was most certainly coddled a fair amount before being kicked out into the real world. In school there was always a schedule, a list of activities, places to go, people to go to the dance with. Heading off to a university was no different, if I'm being honest. Sure, I cried a bit dropping my parents off at the airport after move-in day but my life was still pretty safe and structured for those next four years while I got a bachelor's degree. If you think about it, the North American bubble offers a lot of safe options that "protect" you from having to really understand what's going on. You work in your typically structured job, learn how to pay rent and avoid moving because you "hate packing," and go to the same restaurants and bars because you like the feeling of being a regular. Humans are creatures of habit. Change is hard, yes, but we do these things primarily out of fear. Not in the fear-for-your-life kind of way, but in the fear-of-the-unknown way. The other definition of fear is "the feeling of anxiety concerning the outcome of something." We humans hate not knowing what comes next. We love habits and routines because if we do the same thing all the time, we won't have to deal with any surprises. The outcome feels like it's guaranteed simply because we've done it before.

For example: I'm guessing at least one of the following words instills a mild sense of panic or confusion in you: mortgage financing, 401k, retirement plans, or student loan repayment. Why? **Because you probably don't know anything about it, or even where to begin.** Getting control over your financial future is extremely important, but most of us avoid the topics at all costs and feign apathy just because it seems so intimidating. Traveling full-time in a non-vacation setting can often feel the same way. Those who don't travel are just as curious as the rest of us, but fear is the one thing holding them back. It's why vacation packages and cruises sell so well - we'd rather someone else sort out the details so we don't have to stress about it. There's nothing wrong with just going on a two week holiday. Sometimes I like to check out mentally, too. But if you aren't just dreaming about a vacation, it's because you're interested in that feeling of uncertainty. You actually **want** to feel uncomfortable. Who created your habits and routines - you, or the people and lifestyle you grew up in? Would you even know the difference?

The Happiness Seeker

Right before I began my international travels, I was diagnosed with acute depression. It was a complete and total shock - I actually asked the therapist if I could take the assessment again. Since we don't really know each other, I am one of those never-stops-smiling, borderline obnoxious extroverts who seems to be just as interested in talking to walls as I am with fellow humans. Also, I'm a pretty privileged and lucky gal in the family, friends, and economic predisposition department. How could someone like me have depression?

The thing they don't tell you in that picture book about puberty is that growing up also entails some pretty dark mental journeys we aren't always equipped to handle. Becoming comfortable in a routine often prevents us from processing everything that happens to us and the people in our lives. If the day-to-day looks the same, our brain isn't triggered to respond to things that may actually be abnormal and require some extra feeling. Anything can hide beneath the surface and start building a home there - insecurities, grief, lack of deep connections, failures. Most of us have these storms brewing and we don't even notice them until our house is flipped over and there is a cow in the gas station.

When this happens, your mind will start to wander. You'll get overly emotional at seemingly innocuous stories and details that remind you of what you're actually dealing with deep down. You'll study people whose lives are completely opposite from your own, wondering if the answer lies in dropping everything and getting a fresh start. As you can imagine, fixing that mental destruction takes some time, and your body is going to crave some serious healing if you've let it go on for too long. Asking yourself to process that while staying in the same routine? Well, that's what got you here in the first place.

So if that little voice in your brain is begging to see the world - listen to her. It may not be that she wants pad thai in Chiang Mai. It could be more likely that she wants you to finally open Pandora's box and admit to what's been holding you back. You won't find happiness because you're leaving your pain behind; you'll give your pain room to breathe and the attention it deserves. Happiness seekers end up being the most exhausted travelers, but they have the most to gain.

The Hopeless Romantic

Of course, I have to acknowledge the elephant in the room. I know that one of the not-so-subconscious reasons people travel is because they're looking for a new sea to fish in. In the spirit of transparency, I started traveling upon a rather sudden exit from a serious six-year relationship, so I get it. Whether you're prompted by heartbreak, boredom, or years of frustration, meeting new people is one of the greatest joys of traveling, and also a great way to meet new potential partners as well. However, if you're currently hoping to find love, get married, and never come home, I'm more worried about what you may be covering up.

The thing is, you can only find a true soulmate if you actually know your soul. I know, I know, I promised not to be meta. Let's talk about something universal instead: pizza. Say you grew up eating cheese pizza, and you love it! It's so fresh, so simple, so cheesily delicious. You meet someone, and turns out, they also love cheese pizza. Well I'll be darned, you two have so much in common! You agree to try being dairy-eating carb partners forever. But then one day, your trusty pizza delivery man accidentally slips a piece of veggie pizza into the box.

What is this atrocity? Where is the familiar, clean slate of cheese pizza you are used to?

Being the curious human you are, you decide you are willing to experiment, and take a bite.

All of a sudden, you are experiencing a harmonious symphony of flavors - the popping of a sprig of broccoli, the squish of warm tomato, the salt of a black olive. It's incredible! So incredible, you share it with your cheese-loving partner, as surely your soulmate will have the same experience as you.

Your partner bites and quickly cringes at the symphony you were just relishing. "How are you enjoying this?" they ask. "Let's just eat the cheese pizza."

You stop in your tracks. Of course, before this moment, you were perfectly happy with cheese pizza. But now you want something more. It's all you can think about, and it's shocking that your partner doesn't agree. Of course, you could always order separately from now on, but what else are you missing out on? Could someone else have a different taste that better matches yours, or exposes you to something even better?

If you followed that metaphor, then I think you get what I'm poking at. You can only find your ideal match if you know what you're looking for, and you can't always know exactly what that is if you never leave the confines of the familiar. It's possible for you to learn things about yourself from other people, from comparing your knowledge and tastes to theirs, seeing the world through their eyes. The only thing you need to watch out for is your objectivity, or lack thereof. As humans, it's easy for us to fall prey to the psychological phenomenon known as "mirroring," where you subconsciously start imitating the gestures, speech patterns, and attitudes of those you are close with. This can prevent you from retaining a sense of independence, and mask your true feelings on a subject as you try to fit in with those around you. I am all for international exploration, both physically and romantically, but only if you are able to maintain a healthy sense of self-awareness. We're not all ready for that, and it's up to you to decide what you can handle and what you can't. Love is a brilliant thing, but loving yourself should always be your first priority.

The Purpose Discoverer

A study was recently done at the University of California, Berkeley by professor Morten Hansen that explored the difference between passion and purpose, published in his book *Great at Work: How Top Performers Work Less and Achieve More.* Hansen surveyed 5,000 employees and managers and looked to see which factor correlated most positively with job performance. The employees were grouped into a grid. Unsurprisingly, those employees who lacked passion and purpose were ranked in the bottom 10th percentile by their managers. Those with both passion and purpose, naturally, ranked in the top 80th percentile. That sounds intuitive, right? The real shock comes from which factor is stronger. Interestingly, those with high passion and low purpose scored **in the bottom 20th percentile** of the rankings. The workers who were insanely passionate about their work were virtually useless, not because they didn't care, but because they didn't have a purpose. On the other hand, those with purpose and no passion ranked in the 64th percentile - 44 percentiles above their passionate purposeless counterparts.

	HIGH PURPOSE	LOW PURPOSE
HIGH PASSION	80th Percentile	**20th Percentile**
LOW PASSION	**64th Percentile**	10th Percentile

Many of us have heard the phrase "Do what you love and you'll never work a day in your life." This is only partly true. You can't just love something; it needs to fill you with a greater sense of purpose. I've dealt with this first-hand. When I first graduated high school, I was convinced that I needed to be a performer. I don't think I ever loved singing enough to pursue it full time, but I did love the feeling my performances brought to the people around me. I was so excited about the pride my family had after my shows, the positive feedback in the local newspapers, the social media affirmations from random acquaintances. I felt like I was bringing joy to other people by performing, and that happiness blinded me from noticing anything else I may have been feeling towards the subject. When I finally got to my conservatory in Nashville, TN, I was in for a rude awakening. I was spending hours rehearsing, studying theory, taking voice lessons, and yet, I wasn't happy in the least. If I was "doing what I loved," why did it feel so terrible and exhausting? Once I was alone with only myself to work for, I realized that I was going to music school for other people, and not for myself. I realized empathy was a blessing and a curse.

One day I was sitting in a study lounge, wildly frustrated by chord progressions, when a friend mentioned there was free food at the entrepreneurship club meeting. I wasn't hungry, but I thrust my sheet music into my bag and practically lunged into the group heading towards the open door at the end of the hall. Before I knew it, I was on a Hackathon team with a clicker in my hand, pitching a student housing project to a local corporate sponsor and loving every second of it. I placed 3rd in my category at Nationals that year, and submitted my transfer application to the university in Boston sponsoring the competition the moment my plane landed back in Nashville. I've been studying business and strategy building ever since.

Whether you love what you do, or wonder what the point of it all is as you drudge through a two hour commute day after day, we all want to feel the impact of what we're doing. No one actually knows the meaning of life, but we all know how great it feels to know you've made a difference, and that your presence had an effect on the world around you. The trick to finding this, I think, is to find your **superpower.**

When people hear that, they often think of tangible skills, and get frustrated with the ones they do and don't have. Think a little bit deeper. For example, I know some of my strengths are my empathy, my curiosity, and my ability to innovate and create things quickly. I *choose* to apply those to entrepreneurship and management, but there are dozens of other ways I could have applied them. For me, creating something bigger than myself and building off the synergy of others fills me with purpose - it wouldn't feel that way for everyone. You decide what matters to you. You decide what your purpose is. But you need to know yourself a bit first, and test out the waters.

••

Hopefully, one or all of the above paths spoke to you, and you have started to think a bit harder about why you want to travel. As I explain the basics and some of the more technical sides of this type of adventure, I'm going to mention the personas above to point you in the right direction. There are dozens of different ways to go on this journey, and my goal is for you to choose the one that's right for you, even if it takes a bit of experimentation up front. I want this book to feel like a Choose Your Own Adventure story - follow the twists and turns that match your needs, and feel free to go back and do it all over again as many times as you'd like.

Chapter 2: The Basics - Work

In a book about wanderlust, most people would first think to start talking about traveling, but you've had enough storytelling to satiate you. Dreaming is wonderful, but I was bred to be 50% dreamer and 50% doer.

When I first started exploring the idea of traveling full-time, I fell for basically every blog and Facebook ad copy out there. (We'll talk about why so much of that content exists soon.) I was convinced that all I needed was a few thousand more Instagram followers and the profits from selling everything I own on eBay to fund 12 months abroad. Well, what those bombshell travel bloggers don't tell you is how much freaking work being an influencer is, and how long it takes to turn a decent profit. Also, turns out you actually need to pay people to take your old Forever 21 tops. Goodwill did give me a loyalty punch card though so, silver lining.

If you're like most post-collegiate Americans, on the low end you probably have student loans to pay, some form of phone bill, and health insurance, not to mention the rent, car, and utilities bills you'll be paying until you pack up. Well, that plus weekly ubers to bars and 2AM chicken finger orders on UberEats. No? Just me?

After feeling disheartened by all of the traveling insta-model unicorns I would most likely never become, I came upon another concept: digital nomads.

Digital Nomad *(noun)—A person who is location independent and uses technology to perform their job.*

Location independent, a.k.a., you can work from wherever, whenever. Eureka! There is hope for us non-internet celebrities yet. I know the term sounds a little pretentious at first, and it is going to continue sounding funny to all your friends and family for a while. However, it's really just a fancy way of saying you are not required to go into an office to do your work. You'll want to start getting used to the term now, as that keyword is your new best friend in all future Google searches and travel planning. It's not all that complicated - the actual hard part is finding consistent paying gigs that allow you to replace your current, non-remote income.

As you might have assumed, before you can feel comfortable traveling abroad, you need to have some form of financial security lined up. We're going to get that out of the way first by answering the question: how do you maintain an income while living and traveling abroad?

Step One: Becoming a Remote Worker

I fell in love with the concept of remote work long before becoming a nomad - seriously, it's the bee's knees. My first job out of school was doing software sales for a marketing company (HubSpot, if you're super curious), and we had unlimited vacation as well as the ability to work remotely when needed. Most of our head sales reps came in the office maybe 3-4 times a month, if that. The superstar saleswoman I worked for now works full-time from a completely different state!

All this is to say, remote work is on the rise, and it may not be as far away as you'd think. If you do computer or phone-based work, you have a different first step than most. As is mentioned in the subtitle of this book, before you march into your manager's office to put in your two week's, ask for a meeting to explain to them what you're thinking of doing. Tell them why you want to travel, and present them with some research on remote work, or telecommuting, so they can be on the same page as you.

Tim Ferriss offers some great scripts for this in his now famous book "*The 4 Hour Workweek*," but here are some other helpful statistics to mention:

- Employers lose an estimated $1.8 trillion in lost productivity each year because of lack of engagement with the job, parents stressed over the cost of child care, hangovers, chronic health problems and more. On the flip side, more than 2/3 of employers reported increased productivity from telecommuters due to a lack of distractions.
- 82% of telecommuters report lower stress levels, 80% report higher morale, and almost 70% reported lower absenteeism.
- In a case study done by Stanford, offering remote work as an option reduced employee turnover by over 50%.
- A report by ConnectSolutions discovered that 54% of respondents say that telecommuting allowed them to accomplish more in the same or even less time than they could in the office.

In many cases, replacing you will be far more inconvenient for your manager than experimenting with you working remotely - but make sure you're worth it. If you've been slacking off due to lack of interest, but think you might still want to keep this gig, now is the time to step it up a notch! People will only want to work with you if it's going to be a good return for them. Also, play to their pain points. Have three people on your team quit recently? Are you collectively struggling to hit sales goals or marketing campaign objectives?

Now, for everyone who is not currently doing computer-based work, I'm going to become your remote career counselor for a minute and walk you through some of your options. Let's discuss a few things. What are you currently doing? Why? Is there a way to earn the same income, or even achieve the same purpose or mission by working online instead? My goal here is to give you an overview of career choices and a place to start - it then becomes your responsibility to do the deep dive and make yourself valuable. I am not going to fake being an expert in all of these industries. I want you to be the expert, and then teach me a thing or two!

First things first - we need to talk about niches. What's a niche? A niche is a narrow but comfortable work opportunity that targets a specialized population or interest. Business buzzwords are fun! To help you understand, here's an example: your niche could be that you are a holistic mom blogger, meaning you write blogs that are centered around the topic of natural living, targeting moms. Another example: you could be a virtual assistant for e-commerce fashion executives in California. Again, you need a specific job, in a specific industry, for a specific kind of person. If you want to succeed in finding your own remote income, you need a niche first and foremost. You don't have to stay in it forever! But *not* having one is going to be painful and result in little to no success because there are thousands of other people who are qualified to do exactly what you do. After all, you're going to start doing one of these jobs because you read it in a book (hai!) or watched a YouTube tutorial - do you know how many people can do that? I do, because they're doing it publicly.

For example - if you were to Google "freelance jobs" or "remote work," you're going to see lots of ads for freelance work sites like UpWork and Fiverr. These sites link employers with ready and able freelance employees for quick and cheap projects. There's just one problem. On Upwork, for example, there are 12 million other freelancers just like you (or better) looking for work. How many jobs are posted a year? 3 million.

Are you okay with getting 25% of a gig every year? Could you live off that?

Good, because a 25% gig isn't real, and in reality, you just have a 75% chance of not making any money at all.

Pick a niche. Make it something you're halfway interested in, or at least something you can learn about quickly. I chose to focus on the performing arts and music education, because it's what I had experience in and it's a topic I'm passionate about. You could be smarter than me and pick an audience with more money… or go for passion and purpose. I'm not judging you.

Follow all the big players in that industry on social media. Start reading their blogs. Go to their conferences. Join their Facebook groups. Once you're done, pick a service you think you'd excel at to offer them that they *need*. Don't decide to become a blogger for your favorite websites, HelloGiggles and Buzzfeed. Those are media websites. They have plenty of people who want to do that, and those people are far more qualified than you are right now. Becoming a content creator who makes Buzzfeed/Tasty style videos for local restaurants owners in Cape Town - now you may be onto something. And your Buzzfeed resume will look so much better when you're done!

Digital Marketing

A good majority of nomads are working in the online marketing space, for two reasons: one, there are many areas to specialize in; and two, basically every functioning business today needs it. This is the vertical I work in, and I love it, but it does require a good amount of education, hard work, and adaptability. Luckily there are many resources out there to teach you the ropes and walk you through booking your first clients.

Wondering if marketing could be a good fit for you? A good marketer is creative, but also loves information and has a good attention to detail. You need to be willing to let your ideas go if the data doesn't agree with you, and be diligent enough to run test after test to prove that you are right (or be willing to be proven wrong).

As a fellow marketer, I am wary of how low the barrier to entry is for this field, and I will urge you to proceed with caution. You will be dealing with people's real businesses, real goals, and real money. Two important things to remember: do not sign up to do something you are not qualified to do, and always charge what you are worth. Failing in marketing comes with the territory, but you only want to go through it in order to learn and improve, not because of a lack of effort or experience. I usually sort the different verticals into levels - to proceed to the next level, I recommend becoming extremely comfortable with the level prior, though it's not inherently necessary. The higher your level, the more you can charge for your services.

Level 1: Social Media

Job titles include: Social Media Coordinator or Manager

Description: For this job, you will be running a company's (or several companies') social media accounts. This includes posting daily status updates and images, working with their marketing team on what to post, and engaging with customers and fans. Social media platforms are very intuitive to understand, and there are many quick and free video tutorials offered by the platforms themselves or digital marketing gurus to get you up to speed on the difference between social media for friends versus social media for businesses. You can't charge too much for this, but most businesses need it, some more than others. The best thing to do is to learn some best practices and book several clients, and sign them all into a social media management tool like Sprout Social or Hootsuite. This way, you can schedule out a week's worth of content in a matter of hours, and assign each client to a certain block of time in your week.

Level 2: Content Creation

Job titles include: Blogger, Copywriter, Content Marketer, Video Marketer

Description: Once you understand the frequency of posts a business needs in your work with social media, you will realize the value of posting something lengthy and high quality to your audiences, rather than a few sentences or an image. There are many different types of content businesses can offer, but they mainly fall into four categories: blogs, educational content, videos, and ads. You do not have to specialize in all forms of content, but it is wise to learn the strategy behind content marketing before you begin. You'll want to look for educational resources on content marketing and content creation, and study what the businesses you'd like to work for are posting. Try and replicate their content yourself to see if this might be a good fit for you. You could have a knack for writing or videography you didn't even know existed! Content is extremely valuable, and if your content proves to be engaging, you'll be able to charge more and more for this service, and even combine it with your social media services. However, It is far more time consuming than social media, so be prepared for additional working hours up front until you develop a good process.

Level 3: Inbound Marketing

Job titles include: SEO Manager, SEO Expert, Google Expert, Email Marketer, Marketing Automation, Marketing Funnel Designer, Inbound Marketer

Description: Social media is a great way to get the word out to audiences, but at the end of the day, a business's goal is get customers, and you can only do that on your own territory. For most businesses, that requires customers visiting their website. Learning how to optimize a website and drive traffic to it requires an entirely different skill set. At this point, you are going to be delving into the more complex realm of inbound marketing: the science of getting people to your website and keeping them engaged in ways that turn them into customers. I always recommend the certification from my former employer, HubSpot's Inbound Marketing

Certification. It clearly explains how to connect good content and a social media presence with a solid website, and how to better understand your customers to sell to them in smarter and more efficient ways. Once you have mastered this, you can become an expert in several verticals. Inbound marketing encompasses SEO (how to improve your rank on a Google search), email marketing and advertising, as well as social media and content creation.

It is here that you will start to learn a marketer's favorite tool: funnels. The word Funnel in marketing describes the series of steps a prospective buyer goes through before they purchase, and it is what marketing campaigns are built on. Being a funnel or inbound marketing expert will help you bring measurable success to a business, and that can result in measurable increases to your income.

Level 4: Google or Facebook Ads

Job titles include: Facebook Ad Marketer, Facebook Ad Planner, SEM Specialist, Google Ad Words Manager, Social Media Advertiser

While Inbound Marketing pushes the need for more naturally-occurring business, and less pushy advertising, the world of digital advertising offers its own new sets of challenges and benefits for those who study them closely. The main platforms to use in this space are Google (including Youtube) and Facebook (including Instagram)'s platforms, although Amazon and the Apple App Store have a growing expert base of niche advertisers as well. Again, as you can see, choosing a niche makes your life easier because of the sheer quantity of information you need to learn to specialize in any of those mediums. I don't recommend that you specialize in all ad platforms. Narrow your focus to one kind of ad, for one kind of business, that ideally doesn't target more than two to three demographic groups.

Level 5: Marketing Strategy

Job titles include: Marketing Consultant, Growth Marketer, Growth Hacker, Marketing Strategist

Description: Once you've been in the game for a while, you can start outsourcing a lot of the previous levels, and start advising people on how to combine all of those services into their overall marketing strategy. At this point, you'll move from working with marketers to working with executives and founders so that you can start integrating your efforts with bigger projects like research and operations. At this point, you become their peer, and can charge an hourly rate equivalent to theirs in exchange. This isn't something you get into lightly, and it doesn't mean you drop your niche. It just means you can offer more services within your industry and demographics, and do more high-level thinking.

Level 6: Marketing Expert/Coach (can teach other marketers)

Job titles include: (Topic) Expert, Social Media Guru, Marketing Thought Leader, Digital Marketing Coach

Description: If you are getting ridiculous results, and have people asking you all the time how you're pulling it off, it's time to start sharing the wealth, and making a little bit of it, too. As you get better and better, it's important to be writing down your results and keeping other people abreast of your hard work. Share some of your tips and see if they resonate - you may have the makings of a future course you can sell, a YouTube series to monetize, or an email newsletter to charge for. This gets into influencer territory, which is hard but worth it in the long run, so stay tuned if this piqued your interest.

Virtual Assistant

If you have read *The 4-Hour Workweek* before, you will have heard of this concept. It's self-explanatory, really - you are doing the work an assistant would, but only tasks that can be done online or on the phone. In 2018, that covers basically everything. You can do anything from booking appointments and placing Amazon orders to doing online research and data entry. What you're willing to do is up to you, and what you get assigned is up to the client! You can book gigs like this yourself, or create a profile on sites like TimeEtc.com, Virtual Assist USA, or Upwork. Most VAs come from areas like India or the Philippines, and depending on the tasks, those hiring are often willing to invest more in an assistant from their home country to do tasks that would be faster for a native speaker and resident to complete.

When you are looking for a virtual assistant gig, start with making a profile on an employment platform and applying for open opportunities. It is possible to find your own job by asking contacts in your network for a referral, or creating a target list of companies and/or executives you'd like to work for. However, there is no guarantee those people will be in the market for a virtual assistant, so it is often easier to start with the folks already looking and see where it takes you.

There are several online courses that assist you with the process of becoming a great VA that I would recommend checking out before you commit. At the end of the day, it's about being as helpful and efficient as possible for whoever you're assisting. If you aren't sure where to begin, this is a great entry level job to kick off your remote work experience, and give you a taste of the different kinds of tasks you could become an expert in. The pay is lower to start and will plateau sooner, but it can open doors and help ease you into the transition before you are ready to commit to something more intensive.

Web/Software Development

Now we're getting into the good stuff! In this day and age, there really isn't a more in demand job than a developer or a programmer. I am not even going to pretend to be an expert in this industry, but like marketing, its options are vast, and require a lot of education and skill up front. Unlike marketing, your skill building will not be as fast.This career path is not for the faint of heart. If you're willing to invest in some high-quality schooling and grueling training hours, it will certainly pay off, but not anytime soon. You'll have to decide what kind of developer or programmer you want to be, and what software language(s) you want to learn. Some are easier than others, and some pay more than others. This is great for those who are used to focusing on a task for hours at a time, who work carefully, and who learn quickly. You can't be easily frustrated by errors or things going wrong, you need to have perseverance and a desire to learn. If you tend to quit when the video game gets hard, for example, this route is not for you. On the other hand, if you have been slowly improving the time it takes you to solve a Rubix cube for the past five years, it could be a good fit.

The elementary school introduction to this world is codeacademy, but the money making skills won't come until you invest in a longer and harder program. I don't mean a twelve-step online course, but something in between a series of YouTube videos and an entire university program. A good mid-level option is a coding bootcamp, like Institute of Code or General Assembly. These programs can be completed in dozens of cities worldwide, and can get you up to industry standards in a certain program faster than learning on your own, as well as provide a solid community and networking opportunities. You can learn smaller subsets with less investment, but then again, so can everyone else. If you only want to learn the basics, I'd look to combine your web development skills with some marketing skills, and sell yourself as a technical marketer rather than a developer. Then they won't ask you all the hard questions.

Design

Graphic design is another career option that comes more easily to some, but if you have the skills and the eye, you can make some good money doing it. The downside to being a designer is that graphic design doesn't hold the same reverence as coding - everybody's a critic. However, you only have to learn the hard way a few times with your ugly graphics to call in the big guns - and one amazing design campaign to have you throwing your money at your favorite designer month after month. As a graphic designer, you will work closely with marketers or internal company leaders, like folks in HR. You'll need to become adept at a design software or two (like Adobe Photoshop and Sketch), and then choose what kind of design you do - are you into ad design, or logos? T-shirts, or packaging? In design you don't really need to choose a specific medium, but you do need to define your style and, you guessed it, your niche.

This one takes some practice and a bit of an innate eye for design to be good at, but it's one of the coolest gigs. The difficulty here is securing payment - customers don't always agree on price when it comes to art. You'll want to be sure you make ironclad agreements with folks before beginning a project, or start listing your services on a platform like Fiverr or 99designs to give you some built-in security. Like marketing, though, you'll outgrow those platforms quickly and want to strike out on your own. Make sure you invest in someone to build out your contracts and invoicing, and have a collections company contact handy.

E-Commerce

Another great online medium to become an expert in is e-commerce, or the business of selling things online. I gave this one its own category because it operates by its own rules, but does have a lot of the same roles as the jobs mentioned above. You can be an e-commerce marketer, designer, or programmer, but you'll want to specialize in that from day one. Trust me, trying to jump from another world to big e-commerce projects will result in a lot of wasted money and some seriously unhappy clients. Thanks to platforms like Etsy and Shopify, you can also be an e-commerce merchant and sell your own wares! You don't even need to make them yourself, you can design products and have them made by fulfillment centers and sent to customers by a dropshipping company (or work with one that does both). Ooh, new e-commerce buzzwords for you to Google.

There is lots of money to be made in e-commerce, but there are also lots of sellers fighting for attention and money. Many of them will be much larger than you. To survive, it's wise to study this alongside studying online advertising, and to stay in your niche (weren't expecting that, were ya?). If you come from the world of retail, or have an interest in product sales or working for a larger online seller one day, this is a great place to be.

Passive Income

This buzzword is the Moby Dick of the remote work community - the infamous revenue that you collect while you sleep. Passive income is a phrase that refers to income that isn't tied to hourly work - it earns itself automatically. An example would be the sale of a product online in a store that emails customers and ships autonomously, or an online video course you built once but that 100 people buy every week. These are the kinds of products that make six or seven figures in a year, and it's something we all want in life. Getting there, on the other hand, is not an easy road.

Most passive income streams are digital products (webinars, online courses, ebooks) or highly automated e-commerce stores. You've probably purchased a few of them - they are products like the Instagram bra, the no-theft backpack, the Whole30 recipe book, or any of the hundreds of online fitness programs. (And yes, I have personally purchased some of these.) As you guessed when you bought it, someone, somewhere is making a heck of a lot of money, thanks to a lot of research on their niche, what and how to spend on advertising, and a half-decent product. You'll hear about this concept as you get started in the nomad world, but honestly, this is not something for beginners. You can try, I commend you for it, but don't rely on it. Personally, I'd wait until you've become super attached to and knowledgeable in your niche before you pounce on this, if you ever do. Nothing would make me happier than for everyone who reads this to be making six figures in a year, but if that's not possible, I'd rather you just get out there and function.

Concept Explained: Travel Influencers

Now I know you're curious about travel influencers, and why this book doesn't focus on them. I am equally fascinated by the concept. Social media influencers are like the Kardashians; appearing to be famous for no reason, but actually supported by an insane amount of business acumen and marketing manipulation behind the scenes. I will preface this by stating pretty clearly that I am not an influencer, and also that I have nothing but respect for what they do. All of my discoveries that I'll quickly explain here were made reading several blogs of said internet celebrities, and meeting a few in person at Paris Fashion Week. After my research, personally I'd rather empower more digital nomads than social media celebrities.

But since you're curious....

Becoming an influencer is hard, yet possible, and can eventually become a full-time job. Influencers start in one of two ways: by building up a following on their own blog, or by building up a following on their social media platform of choice. Ultimately, you'll need both to be successful. Typically, they focus on one medium first. Once they get big enough, they start to grow an audience on multiple platforms as their fans get more committed. The biggest mediums for this are Instagram, YouTube, and Facebook. Becoming an influencer involves **a lot** of content creation until you figure out what sticks, as well as supplementary audience nurturing. You need to follow similar accounts, engage with competitors and fans, and create quality advertising for your ideal sponsors (initially) free of charge. It can take months, if not years, to build a following large enough to gain paid sponsorship or to monetize your fans with some of the passive income products we talked about. The threshold for how many fans is enough depends largely on your age demographic and your niche (she's back), and it's only getting harder as more and more people try their hand at it. You'll need to invest in great photography and videography, test out copy that works, and be ready to post great stuff **two to three times a day.**

Oh, and once that's done, you'll also need to start doing sales and development with partners, book new deals, and coordinate PR campaigns according to your clients' marketing needs. That includes reaching out to dozens if not hundreds of sponsors a day, dealing with complex contracts, and potentially having to hire lawyers and accountants to manage your business.

As you can see, this is *exhausting* and there is a lot of work to be done up front before you'll ever see a paycheck, not to mention all the work on the backend once it's built. But you can't put a salary on celebrity, and with big risk can come big reward. Becoming an influencer is like trying to find the Northern Lights - you shouldn't expect it, but with hard work, dedication, and a bit of luck, magic can happen.

Chapter 3: The Basics - Before You Go

Okay, now that you have your remote gig lined up and have started making headway, it's time to prepare for your tour around the globe. And you thought the work was over once you found a job! Being a digital nomad is great, but it does come with its fair set of challenges - including the fact that you'll now be spending five times the amount of time you used to on planning your housing and mini-vacations. It's better than spending your extra time on Netflix though, right? Actually, don't answer that.

Setting a Budget

This is why we started with the work first. Once you know how much income you can secure every month, it's time to see how far that money will take you. Something that tends to shock people is that in many cases, you can actually *save* money by living abroad. I like the way Matt Kepnes puts it best in his book, *How to Travel the World on $50 a Day*, "When you are home, you don't spend a lot of money per day and neither do the locals where you are visiting. If you know just a few general tips and some location-specific advice, you can always have a first-class experience without paying a first-class price. It's about traveling (as the cliché goes) like a local."

The cool thing about being a digital nomad is that you aren't on vacation - you are living abroad. You will experience the same prices and challenges as any expat (expatriate, a person with a residency other than their native country), and that can either be cheaper or more costly than the lifestyle you're used to.

You're probably expecting me to share a magical travel planning spreadsheet with you at this point, but here's a secret: if the trick to traveling abroad is living like a local, the trick to financing is acting like one too. In this case, my best recommendation is to behave as your most responsible self would at home, within reason. You didn't move to Italy to eat in your apartment every night, nor did you travel to South Africa to skip the touristy and expensive safari. I use a finance tracker, Mint, put all my credit cards on autopay, and get reminders if I overdraft so I don't miss a payment or get hit with fees. Figure out what your means are and learn to live within them. If you are starting off with a smaller monthly income, you may want to start off living in a more affordable area like Spain, Eastern Europe, or the more nomad-friendly regions of Asia like Bali, Thailand, and Vietnam. I can't recommend Matt Kepnes book enough when it comes to choosing a country that matches your budget. He provides a global breakdown with realistic estimates based on how you like to live. There is a full list of resources located at the end of the book. You can also use sites like Expatisan.com or NomadList.com to compare your current living costs with the ones in your dream destinations.

As an example, my typical budget in Europe was to spend no more than $1000 USD on housing a month, and $175 per week on everything else, including groceries, meals, alcohol, and shopping. That's really not as ambitious as it sounds, and it means I get to save all the other money I make in an account for fun adult things like investing, and not-so-adult things like surfing classes and last-minute tickets to see the Harry Potter play in the West End by myself. (Both parts, one day, it was a big deal).

If a spreadsheet is your Patronus, by all means, pivot table away! The main idea here is to not sign yourself up for tracking you won't actually maintain. I would recommend some basic financial literacy; practice notating all of your current expenses somewhere, in a notebook or an app, paying them yourself if you aren't already, and applying for a credit card if you don't currently have one (or several). Get familiar with the way your bank account works and start setting up alerts and becoming more cognizant of how and where you spend your money. Doing rehearsals with this at home will save you a lot of headaches when you start doing things abroad.

Credit Cards

Speaking of credit, let's talk credit cards. It still shocks me how many young people don't use credit cards because of warnings from their parents or fear of racking up endless debt. This is, of course, always a risk when you start playing with credit lines, but the benefits and uses of credit cards when used safely make that risk worth it. Simply put, I would not have survived living abroad without a credit card. You cannot always guarantee your income, and you never know when a big opportunity is going to present itself that costs slightly more than you currently want to fork over in cash - not to mention the refundable deposits I can't afford to lose for 5-7 business days.

When you do ultimately go to sign on the dotted line, don't just sign up for the first card that looks good. The best part about credit cards is the ability to rack up their benefits. Choose a card or two that best benefits your travel needs. Do you always stay in hotels? Sign up for the card with your favorite hotel chain - the recent combination of Marriott, Starwood, and the Ritz programs make it a whole lot easier. If you prefer a truly nomadic lifestyle, you're probably constantly changing airlines and booking Airbnbs - opt for a more multi-use card like the Chase Sapphire Preferred or Reserve, or one of Capital One's two Venture cards. Once you spend a certain amount, you'll qualify for their sign on bonuses, worth anywhere from \$500-\$800 in travel, just for spending money you were already going to spend. A cautionary word: don't forget to pay them off. Maintaining a credit balance that is less than 30% of your limit is okay, but you want to be making monthly payments, and making them on time. In addition to a basic daily finance tracker, you'll want to start using a credit score tracker as well. Many bank accounts and credit cards include monthly score reports as a free service, or you can use sites like CreditKarma.com.

When it comes to debit cards, I highly recommend switching to a bank with no ATM fees or international exchange fees as soon as possible. I am in love with Charles Schwab and will never use another checking account abroad, but many local banks offer similar services in order to compete with the big leagues. Again, research is going to be your best friend, as is asking the hard questions to your banks and friends who currently use them. You want to be on the lookout for low maintenance fees and requirements for avoiding them as well, so you're not getting charged for simply using a checking account, or not having enough money deposited each month. Banks are tricky, but where to set up your checking account is pretty easy to figure out once you know what you're looking for.

Concept Explained: Travel Hacking

When you're choosing travel cards, you'll start to get wooed by all of the amazing options there are, and wonder if you could trick them into giving you all the benefits at once. You're not the first one to have that idea, and the credit card companies know it. It's why they make the offers so tempting. They are betting on you to take a gamble, and lose.

But what happens when you win? This is what pro nomads and business folk call *travel hacking*.

Travel hacking is the fine art of manipulating travel credit cards to earn all of their rewards, without taking a huge hit to your debt-to-income ratio or your credit score. As you may know, there are five major factors that go into your credit score.

It turns out, the number of new credit cards you request only makes up 10% of your total score. Same with the number of accounts you have. FICO high earners (folks with a score higher than 785) tend to hold an average of **seven** credit cards at one time. And you thought having more than one was risky!

As resident travel hacking guru Chris Guillebeau says "It's a common misconception that getting multiple credit cards simply for the signup bonuses is 'gaming the system.' In fact, banks are happy to pay for acquiring customers. These banks purchase millions of miles in bulk from airlines and hotels, then distribute them as signup bonuses and ongoing incentives for their new customers. It's a win-win for everyone involved."

My friends still think I'm reckless and living in debt when I tell them about how often I use travel cards (I actually only have four, thank you), but my score hovers consistently between a 780 and 800, and I get an average of 1-2 free flights or hotel stays a month, if not more. I use NerdWallet.com's comparison to see who has the best offers available and I constantly maintain a "waiting list" of the next card I am going to sign up for once I've earned the benefit on the one I have. You wouldn't leave a dollar on the table, so why would you leave a bonus point behind? Always be sure to sign up for loyalty programs and attach your frequent flier numbers, and never buy something with cash or a debit card if you don't have to. Enjoy this almost exclusively American perk to earn free money while having fun around the world.

28

Travel Insurance

Depending on your age and your relationship with your parents, there is a chance you aren't even thinking about health insurance because you're covered by a family plan until you're 26 (thanks again Mom!). However, if you switched to your employer's plan or are self-insured, you're going to want to do some research into how your plan changes by going remote, part time, or when traveling abroad. Medicare and Medicaid, for example, don't cover emergency treatment outside of the US, so you and your family can incur medical bills out of pocket.

Almost every travel blog ever recommends World Nomads for travel insurance, and I've heard they are great, until you make a claim. Universe willing, you won't ever need to count on that, but be smart. You don't want to be figuring this out in a foreign ER while you're incapacitated. Think about your current health conditions, any prescriptions you have, and the countries you're visiting. If you're staying in a first world western nation and plan on working and not doing any strenuous adventure activities, I wouldn't invest in a costly travel insurance. Medical expenses also tend to cost a lot less in other countries! But just because that country has universal healthcare, don't assume that benefit applies to you, too. If you're heading out to scuba dive across the Philippines and hike active volcanoes, you may want to be sure the company and plan you choose has a low deductible, universal coverage and great customer service. I told you traveling was a valuable lesson in adulting! In summary, don't break the bank with travel insurance, but don't go without it.

Phone Plans

Now that you've spent all this effort lining up a job you can do remotely, you are probably surviving off one thing: access to the internet. It's likely that you depend on the ability to use your smartphone to get online and make calls. You may think to call your current phone company, likely AT&T or Verizon if you're American, and see what their travel options are. Joe, the kindly phone customer service man, will kindly tell you that of course you have travel coverage! You can pay per the gigabyte or pay just $10 a day to have the same data plan you have in the US with no interruptions - so easy! Let's do some quick math.

There are 30 days in a month, meaning you are spending roughly $300 a month, in addition to your monthly phone plan spend. Maybe you think that's normal when traveling internationally - I did my first month abroad. Then I walked into a store to ask the cost of a SIM card in Paris and laughed out loud when they told me it was 20 Euro, aka $25 dollars for even MORE data than I was getting at home for $400 a month.

The one downside with using local SIM cards? You have to change your number. If you're staying in one region for a while, you can usually get away with buying one card that can be used throughout the region, and it'll be boatloads cheaper than sticking with your US plan. Changing your number can make you that mysterious friend who lives abroad, and you can decide which friends and lovers you deem worthy to keep your international digits. Fortunately, your WhatsApp number can stay the same no matter what SIM card you use.

If you're like me, and want to be known as that consistent gal who can always be found at 11PM tucked in with a fiction novel - I recommend T-Mobile. They offer the same international coverage automatically with your regular monthly plan that AT&T and Verizon charge for, and you can keep the same phone number and device you've had since high school. Creatures of habit, remember?

The other option that everyone is talking about is Project Fi, Google's answer to a mobile phone plan. Like T-Mobile, the data coverage in this plan costs the same amount no matter what country you are in, but you'll need to switch to a Google compatible phone to get it (bye bye iPhone). I'm a loyal Apple user, but I do find myself ogling the amazing photos other nomads capture with a Google Pixel.

You may have rolled your eyes at how rudimentary this chapter was, or you may have a dozen questions to Google after reading this. Either way, more power to you! The goal is for you to feel safe and comfortable traveling abroad, and getting these essentials sorted first is the key to letting your inner adventurer run wild.

Chapter 4: The Basics - Traveling

Now that your finances are in order, it's time to talk about how to survive once you're out there in the wild! This isn't exactly the fun part yet, but here are the essential bits of knowledge you'll need to get your bearings once you step off the plane into a foreign land.

The Art of Packing

Packing is a skill we can all admit does not come naturally to virtually anyone. We all consistently forget one important thing on every trip we go on, bring a pair of pants we don't touch all week, and at some point get heavily judged by a TSA officer or fellow passenger in the security line for not realizing your water bottle was still full. You are not alone.

I was never a professional packer, and I still don't follow best practices. I haven't even gotten around to getting TSA Pre (oops). What I can say is that I have traveled the world with no more than a backpack and a carry-on, have easily saved myself $500 in checked bags fees annually, and get can through basically any security line in under ten minutes. What, you don't use your smartphone's stopwatch to compete with other passengers?

Packing is something that gets easier with time, and gets even easier if you take stock of your mistakes. For example, before I ever fully unpack my bag, I always make a mental note of what I forgot, and when I repack, I make another mental note of the things I didn't touch. I put the things I forgot first on my list next time, and I never allow the things I didn't touch to come with me again. It's a bit ruthless, I know, but actions speak louder than your dreams to actually wear that expensive skin-tight dress you never actually felt comfortable in.

I still travel with a carry on, not an oversize backpack. The Bigger Carry-On from Away Travel, to be specific. That's not sponsored, I genuinely love my carry-on and tell basically everyone I meet just how much. This is a personal preference, because I rarely ever stay in a place where having a rolling bag is inconvenient. I also stay for one to two months at a time so I usually only have to pull it out a couple of times anyway. There are a lot of travel bloggers and backpackers out there who will show you YouTube videos of them rolling every shirt, legging, and sock into a suitcase with 47 secret pockets. I won't spoil it for you. Basically, there are dozens of ways to out-pack me, and what bag you bring is up to you! The one thing I will discourage is overpacking. Take an honest assessment of how many pieces of clothing you wear in a two-week period, and then recreate that for the climate you're going to. Seriously, **only bring what you need.** In certain rare situations, you will need to bring specific outdoor gear based on what you're planning to do when you travel, but I can almost guarantee you won't wear anything you bring outside of your standard two-week wardrobe. Once you start getting used to a more minimalist lifestyle, you won't want to go back.

Concept Explained: Capsule Wardrobe

As I was preparing for my first trip, I started to go through my closet and was overwhelmed by the sheer number of items I owned. I only wore about ten of them consistently, and the rest lived only in my dresser or my imagination of that perfect event. I took a hard look at the three pairs of leather leggings in my bottom drawer and decided it was time to make a change.

The world of Pinterest is a magical place, and for a long time, I had been tempted by the idea of a *Capsule Wardrobe*. Coined by the owner of a London boutique in the 70s, a capsule wardrobe is built on a selection of essential, neutral colored pieces that don't go out of style. You then augment the wardrobe seasonally so you stay on trend, and can manage in the varying weather conditions.

In order to make my capsule wardrobe, I called in one of my fashion advisor friends. We laid the entire contents of my wardrobe across my bed and floor. It was important to see all the pieces at once, so that I could easily split them into piles - Love, Maybe, Donate, Trash. I needed to have a third party observer to tell me the hard truth about my third peasant top and those baggy sweaters I stole from my ex; we all have weird clothing preferences that are based in insecurity instead of taste.

Once I had the Love and Maybe piles, we started looking for patterns. Neutral pieces like jeans and simple black shirts were opted in, and then we determined a good color palette based on what I already had. In the fall, that became black, white, grey, light brown and dark maroon. It was important not to choose anything with an intense pattern or hard-to-match color, because it wouldn't easily swap with the other items. I also kept a smattering of my most flattering/sweat effective workout clothes, regardless of color.

Now when I pack and when I shop, I never pick anything that isn't in the capsule. I'm a brand manager so it gives me great pleasure to hunt for pieces that are Capsule™ approved, but it also saves me a ton of money and time. I now invest in high quality essentials that I don't need to keep buying, and I'm more intentional with what I allow to be charged to my credit card.

Language Learning

Before you go abroad, all your nice English-speaking friends will comfort you and tell you how kind foreigners are to tourists. "They speak English everywhere, don't even worry about it!"

Okay, so, we are **very** fortunate that thanks to British colonialism, Hollywood, and a global economy, English is very widely spoken and understood worldwide. It's a great base language to be fluent in when traveling, and will get you pretty far. However, I personally find it to be extremely ethnocentric and honestly a bit rude to not even *attempt* to learn the basics of the native language wherever you travel. It's not that you can't get by with English, a smile, and body language - you most certainly can. You need to understand, though, that that is exactly what everyone is expecting you to do. Thanks to the current political climate, Americans in particular don't exactly have a glowing reputation worldwide, and ignorance of the local language fits right into our international stereotype.

I'm not saying you need to feel guilty for being from North America, nor am I ignoring the difficulty that comes with learning a new language! I am simply reminding you that a little bit of empathy and respect goes a long way.

I recommend grabbing a quick language book and using an app like DuoLingo for 5 minutes a day anytime you head to a new country with an unfamiliar language. The most useful phrases you'll want to learn are how to introduce yourself, how to order food, and how to ask for directions. Learn how to explain what you do in that language, figure out the translations of your favorite foods, and memorize your lefts and rights and any frequently-used street signs or transportation-related vocabulary. If you have that down, you'll be able to survive the great majority of conversations, and people will be much more willing to help you. If they speak back to you in English, don't get discouraged, and be appreciative! It's the thought that counts, and at the end of the day, it's better for you to be able to communicate correctly than it is for you to be fluent in half a dozen languages.

Long-Term Rental Housing

I think the biggest difference between traveling as a nomad and traveling as a tourist is your choice in housing arrangements. When you're on vacation, you have a myriad of options: you can go for the more inexpensive hostels and shared apartments, or you can splurge on hotels, resorts, and plastic bubbles under the stars. Your threshold for spending on these places is a bit higher because you're only staying for a week or two, or maybe just a few days. When you start looking for places to stay for one, two, or six months at a time, things get a bit more complicated.

I have now started to treat the process of finding housing as relocating or subletting in various cities. As a nomad, you'll want to be scanning Facebook groups, asking local friends, or looking for long-term rentals on sites like Airbnb and VRBO. You can live with roommates or you can look for an entire flat by yourself; choose whatever makes you feel most comfortable. Just as you would in a normal housing search at home, check how convenient it is for your commute. Where are the local coffee shops and co-working spaces? Also, check the walkability and public transport options, as well as the safety and cleanliness of the neighborhood. You'd be surprised how much money you can save seeking sublets versus more tourist-centered housing, so search like a local! This will be easier to do in areas where English is commonly spoken, and impossible to do in more isolated or less modern regions. Keep your budget in mind, and pick the best option that will make you feel at home.

Concept Explained: Co-Living

Hostels and Airbnbs are great, but something I struggled with in both types of housing was a lack of relatable community. Everyone has heard horror stories of staying in a hostel, but at the very least, hostels have shared common spaces and activities planned to help you connect with fellow travelers. The problem is, they are travelers, not nomads. Most of them are only staying for a few nights, and they are just trying to see the sights and experience the nightlife. They don't really get why you need to be in the room on a conference call at 9PM, nor are they down to sit in a bookstore reading and blogging for several hours during their 72 hours in a foreign city. I met some very kind and friendly people during my hostel stays, and had some seriously rockstar Airbnb hosts, but I usually found myself feeling isolated and awkward. After about a month of this, I'd had enough. I started looking into co-working spaces in my upcoming cities so that I could choose housing that was near a nomad community. It was then that I discovered the joy that is co-living.

Co-living is one of the big trends for digital nomads, but it's just a modern form of a commune centered around a co-working space. Having lived in a recording studio/shared home for a year, I was completely open to the idea, and immediately fell in love with a house designed for female entrepreneurs right outside of Paris. I moved into the Supernanahouse for two months, and became immersed in French culture and language in a way I never could have experienced in a hotel. I was able to work alongside other creators, and bounce ideas off of women who had the same mindset as me.

I've now lived in three different co-living spaces, and it's my top choice for housing when I travel. I love the sense of community it brings, and the things I learn from my fellow nomads who are all on the same crazy journey that I am. Most spaces offer free events and activities, workshops, teaching opportunities, and more. None of them are perfect, but I'd take a community over a fancy apartment any day.

Chapter 5: Choose Your Own Adventure

We've finally arrived at the wanderlust you've been searching for! Now we get into the fun part, although be warned: organizing travel can be notably *not* fun when it's a requirement for survival. However, being able to literally drop your hand on a globe and jet off with your laptop is one of the most freeing sensations in the world. Since the earth is 71% water, though, let's talk about some more efficient ways to plan your sojourn.

The reason why we talked about your personas in the beginning is so that you could have a more targeted direction once we get to this stage. When choosing a destination, it's important to focus on what you're hoping to get out of your experience there, and what creature comforts you are, and are not, willing to sacrifice up front. It's time to **Choose Your Own Adventure.**

If you're The Explorer....

Your goal is to see the world, and if you're anything like me, you probably already have a list of dream destinations in your mind. They are also probably scattered around the globe, nowhere near each other, and require completely different wardrobes, languages, and planning. But you're not going to let that get you down.

Step one for you is to turn your dreams into a wishlist. I would suggest your list include experiences you are hoping to have in each location rather than it just a big list of city names. You can't do all activities year round in cities so it will inform your planning to know what you're trying to do in addition to where you want to be.

How You Should Work

The thing about exploring is that it takes time - time that you aren't working. In order to "have it all," it's going to be crucial that you schedule out a healthy balance of adventure and work. I suggest working a job where you set your own hours and are working on deliverables. Graphic design, programming, and content creation are ideal for this. You don't want to be tied down with constant meetings in multiple time zones, and you want to have the freedom to work on whichever day of the week best suits your schedule. If you are planning to maintain a consistent schedule with clients, just know that you may have to spend more money doing activities on weekends or on the one day a month you don't have anything scheduled. Your schedule is going to change frequently if you have a lot to check off your list, and that can be tiring. Don't overextend yourself. Balance client deadlines with activities, for example, try not to double-book yourself for an excursion in the last 48 hours before a huge month-long project is due. If you do that, make sure you plan to finish it a week early, to give time for the client to receive it and reach out to you with questions and feedback.

Itinerary Tips

Since you are picking destinations with certain goals in mind, once you achieve your goal, you may start itching to move on to the next thing on your list. When you're traveling full-time, bouncing around locations too often is going to start to take a physical and mental toll sooner rather than later, so be careful! I'd suggest booking yourself for four to six weeks in central zones around the activities you want to do. Are you interested in taking a gondola, eating paella, and seeing the Pyramids? You may want to do a weekend in Barcelona before settling in Venice for a month, and then ending the month with a week's journey to Egypt on your way to Tel Aviv to stay in an apartment with a friend from Birthright for a month. Make sense?

Make a map with pins in every place that you have on your wishlist, and look at the spaces in the middle. Are there any major cities or hubs for nomads? If you're not sure, check out NomadList, or look for digital nomad groups in cities in between to see which ones have the most lively communities. I'd recommend picking five or six base cities that are spaced out across the globe, and then scheduling mini-vacations in between. Also, ask your friends for recommendations and see if you have any connections abroad! Exploring is way more fun with a local, and you'll see things you didn't even realize you were missing.

Suggested Locations

Western Europe Bases: Berlin, Lisbon, Barcelona, Amsterdam
Central/Eastern Europe Bases: Budapest, Prague, Belgrade, Tartu
Asia Bases: Chiang Mai, Bangkok, Ho Chi Minh City, Taipei, Daejeon
Pacific Bases: Ubud Bali, Canggu, Kuala Lumpur, Sydney, Wellington
Latin American Bases: Medellín, Buenos Aires, Antigua, Cancún
African Bases: Taghazout, Cape Town, Luanda, Port Louis

If you're The Patriot....

Your goal is to seek independence from your current life, to get a taste of whether or not the grass is greener on the other side. A taste, though, is different than an entire three-course meal. Traveling can go from exciting to overwhelming very quickly, and if you've been living in a routine for a long time, you aren't going to want to dive too deeply into constant movement too early, or ever! To be honest, I think the healthiest way to live this lifestyle is as slowly as your heart and wallet will allow.

How You Should Work

When you're looking for independence, you want to choose a job with some structure, but more freedom than you're currently used to. I wouldn't recommend jumping into full-time freelance work right off the bat, but would push you to look for a part-time remote gig or ask your boss to let you telecommute and do fewer check-ins. I suggest part-time because I think it's valuable for you to have time to add in some new activities and adventures. I think going full-time in entrepreneurship or self-managed freelance can lead to a lot of anxiety and lost productivity at first for those who have lived in a more sheltered or structured environment most of their life.

Itinerary Tips

When you're talking about slow travel, you're not going to be creating a bunch of destinations to check off on a list. Instead, you need to think about the kind of lifestyle you want to experience. Take stock of your current community and routine. What do you love about where you live? What are you looking to try? Think about the elements of your routine you don't want to lose, and then be ready to embrace the culture you move to for the rest.

For example, you may be curious about taking dance classes, and want to live in a country with great food, but don't want to give up your access to great vegan restaurants and grocery stores. You may love the idea of Asia, but the living accommodations are more isolated, it's a huge culture shock, and dance classes aren't as readily available, so you opt for Medellín in Columbia.

I wouldn't suggest living in a location for less than two or three months, otherwise you will feel rushed and struggle to find stability or a consistent group of friends. If you are initially craving a more active vacation, I'd start off with a planned vacation, either with a tour company or a very popular tourist route like a Western EuroTrip with a lot of easily accessible itineraries to help you stay organized. Once you're done, you can settle in a final destination and focus on occasional day or weekend trips rather than frequently changing locations.

Suggested Locations

(Pick four cities maximum per year, ideally two or three)

Europe: Barcelona, London, Berlin, Budapest, Las Palmas
Latin America: Medellín, San José (Costa Rica)
North America: San Diego, Toronto, Montreal
Asia: Canggu Bali, Ubud Bali, Phuket, Taipei

If you're The Happiness Seeker....

You've lost something very powerful recently, or maybe even a long time ago. Happiness is elusive even for those who seem to be living the dream and traveling the world. The trick to finding happiness is to stop looking for it, and to start seeking clarity around your own thoughts and feelings. In your travels, you want be looking for destinations and lifestyles where you can breathe, and where you can find kindred spirits. While we often want to retreat into ourselves on a solo journey for self-reflection, it's important to strike a balance between quiet meditation and the energy of other human beings. I don't think I've ever lived in a country where I haven't spent at least one or two entire days feeling sorry for myself and binge watching romantic comedies until I fall asleep at 10PM. We all need those days sometimes. However, I found I was my happiest in the moments of peace right after having an amazing conversation, or going on an adventure with someone who was becoming a real friend. It was then that I would realize how nice it was to smile involuntarily, to explore, and to feel connected to another person, even in a small way. Sometimes seemingly generic conversations would remind me of a story from my past I hadn't yet processed, or bring back up a memory of an old pastime I hadn't explored in ages.

How You Should Work

The hard thing about this path is you can't really plan what mood is going to strike you when. I had months and weeks where I was able to finish projects that previously would have taken me a full year, and then I had entire legs of my journey where I worked no more than five hours a week. Be sure that whatever remote work you choose isn't overly demanding, and leave room for flexibility and autonomy. If you have the organization and strength to become your own boss and go out on your own, I highly recommend it for this path. Being able to control when your business grows and when it takes a backseat is invaluable, because it allows your work to match whatever wave you're currently riding.

You will need a fair amount of financial buffer to pull off those ebbs and flows without having to pack up and head home, but you'll feel a lot less guilt and often find unexpected bursts of productivity when you give yourself this freedom. I have also found that taking ownership of a project can give you a renewed sense of strength, and help you pinpoint the areas that are holding you back.

Itinerary Tips

I encourage Happiness Seekers to focus on community and comfortable living more so than isolation or "life-changing" experiences. I have had nomadic friends go through religious ceremonies, skydiving, intensive yoga retreats, and ten-day hikes across mountain ranges without feeling a single serious change in their disposition. Building self-awareness takes time, and it's going to take hours away from your professional productivity as well.

If you're looking to gain some perspective, odds are you have no idea what process you are about to go through, or any clue where to begin. My suggestion is to start easy, and to expect the unexpected. Don't book more than two or three months out at a time. It's okay if you have a specific event or festival you are trying to attend, but mark the dates on your calendar as tentative. Family and friends may try and lure you home with specific events, but don't agree unless they are extremely important. Disrupting your process with familiar triggers and locations can slow down your progress more than your realize. In order to find your bearings and build some hooks in a city, it's going to be important for you to plan to stay in a destination for a minimum of three to four weeks. I wouldn't suggest staying in one place too long; this can leave you in a bit of a stalemate and let old habits sink back in.

As I mentioned earlier, you should seek out a community so you can follow the energy of others and the ideas they spark in you. I have changed my next destination based on one conversation and had the time of my life, so don't be afraid to sign on for something spontaneous. At the same time, you should try to maintain a good sense of self. Make sure your living establishment is comfortable and that you have a space you can go whenever you need it to find uninterrupted quiet. You don't need to say yes to everything. It is perfectly okay to trust your intuition around certain invites and travel plans. The main goal is to stay open-minded and be nice to yourself.

Suggested Locations

(Pick two to three that are within a four-hour flight of each other to start)

Pacific Bases: Ubud Bali, Canggu Bali, Phuket Thailand, Wellington NZ
Central/Eastern Europe Bases: Budapest, Croatia, Tartu Estonia, Latvia
Western Europe Bases: Berlin, Porto, Edinburgh, Amsterdam
Latin American Bases: Costa Rica, Chile, Belize

If you're The Hopeless Romantic....

When you're looking to get out of Dodge and jump into the nearest new ocean, choosing destinations is one of your last priorities. I know most people start thinking about what kinds of people they date, what accents they find attractive, or what cultures tend to be the most romantic. Before you hop on a plane to Paris to find your storybook romance, let's back up a bit.

I have never forgotten this line from one of my favorite romcoms, "Every woman has the exact love life she wants," (*The Wedding Date*). Now, this movie came out in 2005 and of course, romantic comedies are known for perpetuating gender stereotypes, but I think that quote applies universally. Whether you're single and love to complain about it or you're pretending to be in love but questioning it every night, pretty much any romantic problem you're having boils down to some internal issue. The answer to your love life woes aren't in finding that special someone, but in finding out what in you is drawing you to the wrong person, or no person at all.

Most of the time, the problem you're dealing with has nothing to do with another person. Hopeless Romantics actually have a journey that's pretty similar to the Happiness Seeker, only romantics will blow me off if I push alone time too much. To be clear, I'm not against traveling for love, because how you react to other people can reveal a lot of unexpected truths about yourself. I just want to clarify that this process isn't about finding a soulmate, it's about figuring out who you need that soulmate to be.

How You Should Work

If you're looking to connect with other people when you travel, be sure that the job you have doesn't keep you too isolated. If you always have to be on client calls and work in a different timezone, you're going to spent most of your time in quiet rooms by yourself. That kind of work is holding you back from great mid-day conversations at the coffee shop or evening lunches with a group of new friends from the co-working space. At the same time, I wouldn't take on a huge solo project or start a new company unless it's in something you are already very adept in. That kind of work also requires a heavy time commitment and focus, and the business (aka your income) will suffer when you get distracted. Working for another company doing consistent work is your best option here, especially if you have the opportunity to network with other employees! It's good to keep your social muscles flexed, and to keep your mind active when you're seeking self-exploration and human connection.

Itinerary Tips

The tough thing about international dating is the inconsistency. Many expats or people on dating apps are often only in town for a short while and any connection you make can be cut short. Don't fall for something when the "timing is off." Find your bearings in a city and really dive in to the community! Pick a location which has a similar culture as your own, or that you have studied a bit so that you feel comfortable going out in local establishments as well as in hubs for other travelers. I would push for very extended stays of four to six months at a time so that you have the ability to get adjusted before you start putting yourself out there. You'll also be able to meet more locals and residents this way who have time to go out on the town with you more than once or twice.

You also might want to pick a location that puts you a bit out of your comfort zone. I find that the more familiar the environment, the less likely you are to grow and take risks. There is a reason your love life has gone stale, and you want to be sure you are almost forcing yourself to spice it up and increase your stress hormones so you actually have fun and are open to romantic connections. Pick a country that speaks equal amounts of English and a more local language, or an up-and-coming city with a lot of international company relocations. Don't go for the romantic destination failsafes. Take it from a girl who's done it: not even Paris is going to resuscitate your boring dates.

Suggested Locations

Western Europe: Lisbon, London, Amsterdam, Las Palmas
Central/Eastern Europe: Krakow, Estonia
North America: Mexico City, Denver, Austin, Toronto, Vancouver
South America: Buenos Aires, São Paul, Chile
Pacifica: Sydney, Ho Chi Minh City, Bali, Daejeon
Africa: Taghazout

If you're The Purpose Discoverer....

Let's not beat around the bush: purpose is a big idea to discover, and I'm not going to try to sell you on a magical destination or three-month itinerary that is going to reinvigorate your sense of self and change the world. I'm not a Miss Universe contestant. However, I think the secret to finding a good purpose to work towards at any given moment is via experimentation and curiosity. I find the best way to discover your purpose is to figure out what makes other people tick, and follow whichever stories spark the biggest fire in you when you hear them. Doing this is going to require a lot of talking and a lot of exploring, but that's the point of this life, right?

How You Should Work

While it will be important to maintain a steady stream of income in some form or another, since you are looking to try new things, don't commit to anything too soon. You want to be able to set aside whatever you're working on to a join a retreat for a few days, or work a few shifts at a local community theatre you learned about through a girl in your yoga class. If you have the ability to save up a good chunk of money beforehand, I'd recommend it in this case to make you more flexible. I'd also start looking into expanding your skill set with whatever steady income stream you pick up. Don't do the same thing you already know how to do because it's safe. Challenge yourself to fund your lifestyle with a new career opportunity, which could bring you down a path closer to your purpose as well.

Itinerary Tips

Where you go on this destination completely depends on what life throws your way, and there's no easy way to plan that.

While I don't usually encourage a lot of strict planning for self-discovery, in your case, I'd push you to put together a string of certain festivals, community events, or volunteer opportunities to structure your travel plans. It can be hard to find a purpose when you're working aimlessly on projects just to earn an income and staying in one place all the time. You need to be challenging your mind and experiencing things you would not have tried before.

If you're looking to find your purpose, try to find places where people inspire you. If technology fascinates you, go to big tech hubs or find co-living spaces that run development workshops and hackathons. If non-profits and volunteering are speaking to you, seek (safe and actually helpful) opportunities to give back and earn your housing in exchange for sweat equity. When you're on the hunt for a purpose, no job is too small and no class is too random to sign up for. You'll find inspiration in the strangest of places.

I would suggest planning out a starting destination with a one-way ticket, and seeing what happens from there. A bit reckless, I know, but I think to find what truly drives you, you really need to take your everyday thinking brain out of control. Where you start is mostly irrelevant as long as you can afford it. You'll meet people who can point you in several different directions - don't pick anything too touristy or too isolated. You want it to be easy for you to plan step two once you find it.

Suggested Locations

Europe: Iceland, Amsterdam, Belgrade Serbia, Budapest
Asia: Chiang Mai Thailand, Kuala Lumpur Malaysia, Ho Chi Minh City Vietnam
Latin America: Medellín, Antigua, Lima Peru

Chapter 6: The Catch

I know that traveling full-time, working remotely, and taking control of your life sounds like a fantasy. It probably feels closer than ever now that you've read this book and started to realize that for thousands of people, that dream is a reality. And it can be for you, too.

Until you don't want it to be.

But AJ! What are you talking about? You just spent literally thousands of words telling me exactly how, why, and where I need to travel. Why would I go through all of that to give it up?

It's hard to explain. I was afraid to talk about it openly for a while, because it felt so privileged and bratty to express discontent with my current lifestyle. If I ever asked other nomads if they were happy, they'd stare back at me blankly, giving me the same cookie cutter response they tell themselves every day. "Of course I'm happy. How could I not be?"

I think somewhere between the 1950s and today, we were bred to distrust the comforts associated with building a home. We don't want to be housewives making a different flavor of pie every week and getting over excited about owning a television set. It's 2018, gosh darnit! We cut cable! We work remotely! I can have 14 world cuisines delivered to my door in 30 minutes or less! This isn't Pleasantville - go roam the world, write your blog, and shut up.

I think that as full-time travelers, we have a fear of standing still. We think, "if I were anywhere else, I would just dream of traveling. It's wasteful for me to go home." That age-old cliché about greener grass starts floating to the top of our mind, but it's quickly sucked out of headquarters and out-reasoned by the joyful wandering child ruling our thoughts. Living this life can sometimes feel like the pinnacle, like you've finally reached self-actualization and that there is nowhere to go from here but up!

I recently came upon a study about Japanese tourists which described a unique phenomenon they experience known as "Paris Syndrome." In Tokyo, for example, the streets are filled with French patisseries and French fashion retail outlets like Chanel and Louis Vuitton, prompting an obsession with French culture that pushes six million Japanese tourists to visit France every year. Upon arrival, though, most of these tourists enter a form of culture shock and disappointment with the city of lights that is so extreme it causes hallucinations, sweating, anxiety, and depression.

I find it unsettling that I can relate to these disheartened travelers. I am living my dream, but it doesn't make my spirit soar every day like I expected it too. There are more days then I like to admit where I fantasize, not about seeing worldly destinations and soulmates, but about house decor, adopting a dog, and returning to the same local bar with my friends every Friday. I rarely every admit that to people, and I'm not sure why it makes me so scared. It's not homesickness, it's not culture shock, it's just a realization that habits aren't exactly the antithesis of unhappiness - not expressing yourself is.

I would never change my nomadic experience. I am so grateful for my world travels, and I don't think I'll ever approach travel or vacationing in the same way again. But I don't think I'm as afraid of myself as I used to be; I'm not afraid of losing myself. Traveling has opened my mind to new perspectives, introduced me to incredible people and places, but more importantly, it has given me a better understanding of how to take care of myself. I know how to spot the warning signs of discontent, how to challenge myself, how to seek new ideas and shake up my expectations.

Now that I know what's possible, I feel more comfortable admitting that I don't need to travel all the time to be happy, and that I am the only person whose opinion matters on the subject.

I hope one day you start to feel that, too. You can take a lot of things from this book, and it would make me so happy if you did. Something pulled you to this page, and I hope a whole bunch of feelings are going to keep pushing you around the world. If you only take one thing from this, my best advice is to enjoy the ride as much as you can, and to never silence the ideas of the most important person in your life: you.

About The Author

AJ Marino is Boston-bred adventurer on a mission to explore the confines of what it means to be happy at work. A self-diagnosed workaholic, she can always be found dreaming up a new scheme, sketching out a business model in a notebook, or telling you about her latest blog idea. AJ currently runs a sales and marketing agency, Intrinsic Marketing, focused on helping arts education companies and non-profits monetize their fans and sell new products. She is equal parts cat and dog person, and is ideally going to be traveling the world full-time as a digital nomad until becoming a full-time MBA candidate in the Fall of 2019.

Follow her on Medium, Intagram or at read more on her website, meetajmarino.com

Acknowledgements

This book is a labor of love and a product of the inspiration of co-working spaces. Thank you to Restation for organizing an amazing productivity camp, and to my fellow Gran Canarian nomads for cheering me on. I'm also thankful to everyone who ever commented, shared, liked, or messaged me questions and support about my blog and my travels. You all were my inspiration to write this book, and I hope it is the first of many things you inspire me to create.

I want to send so much love to my Mom and Dad for encouraging me to dream, teaching me to be independent, and not asking too many questions when I said I wanted to buy a one-way ticket to Europe.

To all my friends back home who answer my endless Facetimes requests, laugh at me when I complain about being depressed on the beach, and help me feel much cooler than I actually am – thank you. You are my family and I will always return the favor of your endless empathy and kindness.

Also thank you to every other writer who shared their knowledge on the internet about self-publishing a book – you rock.

Appendix A

Reading List

While I was never able to find a comprehensive guide on how to take a journey of self-discovery, I did find multiple novels and how-to guides that I wouldn't have been able to live without. In case you want even more knowledge before you go, here is my recommended reading list.

The 4-Hour Workweek: Escape 9-5, Live Anywhere, and Join the New Rich

Author: Tim Ferriss

Blog: fourhourworkweek.com

Buy it on Amazon or wherever books are sold

How to Travel the World on $50 a Day: Travel Cheaper, Longer, Smarter

Author: Matt Kepnes

Blog: www.nomadicmatt.com

Available on Amazon and Barnes & Noble

Conquering Mountains: How To Solo Travel the World Fearlessly

Author: Kristin Addis

Blog: www.bemytravelmuse.com

Available on her website only

The Ultimate Guide to Travel Hacking

Author: Matt Kepnes

Blog: Nomadic Matt

Available on his blog only

Lonely Planet Travel Guides

Author: Lonely Planet

Blog: LonelyPlanet.com

Buy them anywhere travel books are sold

Appendix B

List of Co-Living Spaces

Sun and Co

Location: Javea, Spain

Sun and Co. is the first coliving and coworking community in the whole Mediterranean Coast. A place for freelancers, entrepreneurs, location independent workers, digital nomads and anyone looking for a great work and leisure balance. Sun and Co. is formed by like-minded people sharing living and working space, ideas and fun.A real co-living experience with all under one roof in a 19th-century house located in the center of Jávea, a historic seaside town in Spain.

Website: sun-and-co.com/

SunDesk

Location: Taghazout, Morocco

SunDesk is a coworking and coliving community located in the sunny surf village of Taghazout, Morocco. The SunDesk coworking space is on the second and third floor of the building, and offers amazing ocean view from all desks. Their office can host a maximum of 14 coworkers. SunDesk provides a pleasant, quiet place to stay located next to the coworking office, with both private and shared rooms (with another coworker) available. All of their co-living rooms are located in shared flats with a well-equipped kitchen and a cosy living area for relaxing, socialising, and eating. When it's time to take a break, check out the surf, or just relax, our terrace offers a stunning view of Taghazout and the ocean.

Website: sun-desk.com/

CoCo Hub

Location: Malta

The most colorful place to #getshitdone in the Mediterranean. In one of the most beautiful areas of Malta, CoCoHub has created an inspiring working and living environment. Who needs motivational quotes if you are staying in one of the most welcoming and beautiful communities with the 24/7 ability to grind? CocoHub can host up to 16 remote workers in their 400 square metre mansion, and they offer both shared and private co-living spaces with laundry, a kitchen, and backyard access.

Website: cocohub.io

Mokrin House

Location: Serbia

Mokrin House is a coworking and coliving space located in the north of Serbia. It is a modern and urban spot in the rural surrounding. Mokrin House's ergonomic campus is a perfect place for freelancers, entrepreneurs and digital nomads, who are looking to getaway from the big cities and enjoy living and working in the countryside, for 2 weeks, 2 months or 2 years. They provide you with three meals a day, private rooms, and are constantly hosting workshops, educational seminars, cooking classes, and more.

Website: mokrinhouse.com

Outpost Club

Location: New York City

Outpost club is an end-to-end housing service that offers a networking of co-living homes throughout bustling New York City. They make the process of moving to New York easy and affordable, while offering the opportunity for community and professional networking.

Website: outpost-club.com

Swiss Escape

Location: Grimentz, Switzerland

Swiss Escape is the first coworking and coliving space in Switzerland for freelancers, entrepreneurs and teams that are looking to get closer to nature. It is composed of two chalets which welcome up to 15 people, complete with kitchens, lounges, and ski storage. They offer a shared co-working space and regularly organized business talks, social dinners, and ski and hiking excursions.

The Collective

Location: London, UK

The Collective is a luxury co-living option, providing quality, modern and serviced apartments, studios and rooms in some of London's most iconic locations. All guests have access to the well designed co-working spaces which also serve as event hubs in the busy London professional community.
Website: https://www.thecollective.com/mission/

Outsite

Locations: California, Hawaii, Costa Rica, Lisbon, Bali, NYC, Austin

Once you become a paying member of the Outsite community, you have access to their high-end co-living spaces scattered across popular nomad destinations worldwide. They offer shared and private rooms in all-inclusive homes, with community co-working spaces and organized activities. They are constantly adding new locations and offering exclusive deals and events to their growing membership base.

Website: https://www.outsite.co/

Restation
Location: Las Palmas de Gran Canaria, Spain

I of course needed to include this little spot on the list, as it is the entire motivation behind this book! Las Palmas is a small city on the coast of the largest Canary Island. Once a hub for European retirees, it is now a thriving digital nomad community. Restation is one of the co-working spaces on the island, and they also offer several apartments for co-living as well.

Website: http://restation.co/

Selina

Locations: Cancun, Mexico City, Costa Rica, Panama, Antigua, Nicaragua, Medellin, Ecuador

Selina is a co-living and co-working network with more than a dozen locations throughout Latin America. Home to nomads, travelers, and explorers alike, they offer beautifully designed accommodations, and a strong energy in the urban centers they are a part of.

Website: selina.com

Appendix C

Resources for Future Nomads and Explorers

I mentioned quite a few links and resources throughout this book, and I don't expect you to remember all of them! Feel free to use this Appendix as a resource when you begin your research.

NomadList: nomadlist.com

Hashtag Tourist: Convincing Your Boss to Let You Be a Digital Nomad

Airbnb: Subletting with Airbnb

Homeaway: Large, long-term rentals

WWOOF: Live and learn on organic farms worldwide

Trusted HouseSitters: Free housing in exchange for pet and house sitting.

Facebook Groups

Digital Nomads Forum

Digital Nomads Around the World

Digital Nomad Girls (My personal favorite!!)

Housing for Digital Nomads

All co-living and co-working spaces, as well as cities will have their own Facebook groups – don't forget to join them before you go! And introduce yourself – I promise it's not that weird.

Work Training Resources

HubSpot: Inbound Marketing Certification

Hootsuite: Social Media Management

Udemy: Online Courses in Marketing

Skillshare: Marketing Classes from Industry Leaders

Institute of Code: Web Development Bootcamp

General Assembly: Coding, Data, Design, and Marketing Training Programs

Facebook Blueprint: Facebook Advertising Certification

Google: Adwords Certification

Freelance Platforms

Upwork

Fiverr

99Designs